Poetical Sketches
of St Ives

Poetical Sketches of St Ives

by

Sarah Nichols

Hollyman Press

CONTENTS

To my husband, Peter,
for sharing St Ives with me.

To mum and dad, who first introduced us to St Ives
and who love it as much as we do.

To Penny, my sister,
and to Maureen, Peter's mum.

Introduction

I have visited St Ives for the last few years with my husband, Peter, usually in September, but also during quieter times in March. It was whilst I was on holiday in St Ives that I began writing poetry and my first poem was *'A September Day in St Ives'.*

I have written this small book of poetry for myself and Peter, to remember the good times, experiences, sights, smells, noises and feelings we have already shared in St Ives and, hopefully, can look forward to in future years.

I hope it will also bring pleasure to people who have visited or live in St Ives, and also to others who may be inspired to go there sometime in the future!

There are many wonderful artists working in St Ives and, unfortunately, I cannot paint or draw at all. I have therefore called my book *'Poetical Sketches of St Ives'* as I have tried to capture in words and images, what I can't capture on canvas.

I hope, however, that the poems are more than a static photo, or a single picture, and that instead each one forms a short story. I have tried to create movement and feeling within the words and to convey this to the reader.

These poems are written, above all, to share and to be read aloud, either while you are on holiday in St Ives or once you have returned home and are desperately trying to hold on to those memories!

I hope you enjoy this journey through St Ives by day and by night, in sun and in rain.

Sarah Nichols

Looking out from our flat on The Wharf towards the harbour beach, we were mesmerised by the antics of the many dogs – all shapes and sizes – let loose by their owners onto the sands.

If you have a dog and have never visited St Ives in March, I recommend that you pay it a visit. The weather may be stormy, windy, rainy and cold, but your dogs will have a marvellous time, racing over empty beaches, tearing after seagulls (but never catching them!) and chasing each other into a freezing cold sea.

Dog Days

*'Dogs prohibited on the beach
from Easter day to October.'*
But today is a squally,
mad-March morning:
a perfect sea dog day.

A rag tag bag
of mongrel mayhem
erupts on to the placid sands;
tearing and haring,
racing and chasing,
skirmishes into the sea.

The tumble and scruff,
bluster and bluff
of an over-exuberant pup;
cavorting and sporting,
gliding then colliding
headlong into a wave.

Dogs ambling,
dogs shambling,
most of the dogs gambolling;
dogs loping,
dogs loafing,
an odd dog alone moping;
dogs yapping,
dogs scrapping,
seagulls alarmed flapping:
all gathering down at the bay.

*'Dogs prohibited on the beach
from Easter day to October.'*
So look out for a squally,
mad-March morning:
a perfect sea dog day.

Sitting in *'Cobblestones'* café our gaze was drawn, as usual, to the wonderful view out of the window across the bay and towards the lighthouse. In this poem I have tried to recreate not only the view, but also my feelings as the fog rolled in…

As the Fog Rolls in

Looking out across the bay
the world begins to dim.
As the fog rolls in
the coast fades out,
the houses falter,
the lighthouse fails.

As the world gets smaller
my thoughts grow larger,
what lies beyond the pale?
Not a sound except
the grinding waves,
all colours a toneless grey.

Like a painter who wants
to start again,
to redefine his landscape.
He plunges his brush
in a swirl of water
and washes his canvas over.

A sudden surge of panic,
a fleeting flash of fear
before
the fog thins out
and the world streams through
brighter than it was before.

Porthminster is a very popular beach and although it is great to visit during the day, mixing in with the hubbub of sandcastles, cricket, paddling, sunbathing, volleyball, swimming, picnicking … we like to walk along it in the early evening once everyone has gone home.

Telltale signs of the visitors remain, however, for a short time, giving an intriguing, if fleeting, glimpse into their lives…

Footsteps at Porthminster

So many lives criss-cross over the sand,
here today, gone today:
large feet, small feet,
running feet, baby feet,
heavy feet, light feet,
patterned feet, trainered feet,
big toes, heel, toe,
pushchair trail,
footstep Braille.

Seagulls three-pronged pointing toes,
where do their inverted arrows go?

Everyone knows that George woz 'ere
September two thousand and three.
Skirting round the Pete hearts Soo,
sandy signatures skilfully scribed:
we all want to leave our mark.
Happy Birthday Amy!

Up above the high tide mark
in the grimy fag-ash sand,
the trash-can trails of straws, of glass,
a polystyrene cup, a tyre.

So many lives criss-cross over the sand,
here today, gone today:
transient life-lines washed away,
a blank canvas for another day.

Carbis Bay is a wonderful place to be, especially when it is empty! All you can see is untouched sand, stretching out before you, pitted now and then with the odd shell.

I still like to collect shells and always end up back in St Ives with my pockets full of them. I find it strange this fascination we have with something that is dead and left washed up on the beach, no longer of any use. Is it the shell shapes, the colours, the fine detail or the pleasure of collecting that makes us walk the beach eyes fixed on the sand, searching out perfect specimens to take home and treasure?

Shells at Carbis Bay

Mother of pearl swirl,
a periwinkle twist
washed ashore alone
upon a stretching beach,
dragging at the sand,
out of water's reach.

Finely crafted on the outside
but empty deep within;
its delicate, fragile beauty,
chipped and water worn,
reveals a death far out at sea,
many years ago.

Picked up by an inquisitive child
not really understanding,
and stored in his collection,
wrapped up in cotton wool,
brought out on special occasions
to show to favoured friends.

Walking from St Ives to Carbis Bay when there's a mist veiling both land and sea is exhilarating. Although you can't really see anything you can feel the damp air in your hair, soaking through your clothes, sending a shiver of anticipation down your spine.

I'm not really sure why sea mist makes me think of mermaids; perhaps it's the thought that when you can't actually see the sea, only hear it, you don't know what could be out there…

Mermaid Through the Sea Mist

The light cold touch
of still, salt air
sculpts the sugar strands
of her filigree hair
into finely twisted curls.

*The sea mist wreathing
its aura of mystery
around her head.*

Water-logged ringlets
coil heavy
about her cheeks,
snaked through
with suspended droplets.

*The sea mist seething,
the sea mist wreathing
its aura of mystery
around her head.*

Tangled wisps weave
like a spider's
gossamer threads
into intimate
secret passions.

*The sea mist breathing,
the sea mist seething,
the sea mist wreathing
its aura of mystery
inside my head.*

This poem is based on a photograph of my mum standing in the rain on Carbis beach. Not a particularly flattering photo as she is wet and bedraggled, but one that conjured up a vivid picture for me: the sudden dash for childhood that I make when I'm alone on a beach and the weather is wild and stormy; the feelings of rebellion against convention and the urge to run madly along the beach letting the full force of the rain and the sea spray beat against my upturned face.

Alone on Carbis Beach

Glasses peppered
with a salty rime,
I'm bespattered
and begrimed,
my jacket soaking wet.
I've made a dash
for freedom
over deserted sands.

No umbrella
of respectability
to save me
from the rain.
Galloping along
the empty beach,
hair crystallised
by the brine.

The wind coursing
through my emotions,
the sea
swirling inside
my mind
like the roar
inside a shell,
I feel excitement swell.

My gaze lost
in the horizon,
sand splashes
up bare legs.
Regression
or progression
to a second
carefree youth.

For this poem, I tried to imagine what it would be like
for someone who was very old living by the sea;
someone with time on their hands, and who spent a lot
of it watching the sea.

Looking Out Towards the Sea

I'm ninety-three,
live on my own,
and all my friends have died.
But I'm not at all lonely
as I sit on my own
looking out towards the sea.

Always a reason
for watching,
no one wondering
why
I'm sitting on my own
looking out towards the sea.

An acceptance
it's the thing to do,
an old woman
on her own,
coffee cup in hand,
looking out towards the sea.

No awkwardness because
I'm on my own,
as I am occupied
by the sea
which swirls through
the empty hollow
deep inside of me.

When my husband and I first saw dolphins in the bay at St Ives, I think we were more excited than the children! You could actually feel a thrill go through the people around us as they realised what was out there amongst the waves. All around us men (including Peter) were diving for their binoculars as the women (including me!) were waving their arms feverishly towards the open water, making strange squeaking noises of delight.

In this poem I've tried to capture that sudden excitement as the dolphins arrived, gave us a quick show and then sped off again.

Dolphin Dance

A Mexican wave of binoculars flashes around St Ives
as people stare far out to sea with bright, excited
eyes,
The dolphins are approaching, swimming right in to
the bay,
*'Quick, look out towards the sea, don't miss the
dolphin display!'*

'Look! A school of dolphins,' a clever body cries,
but I'm not quite sure that the wise word 'school',
really should apply.
Dolphins they have too much fun, playing the watery
fool,
to belong to anything I know of as orderly as a school!

With a flash of flippant fin,
a crash of flailing tail,
a sudden blow of air,
they leave a frothing trail.

Like horses on a merry-go-round
up and down in time.
Then an all-engulfing splash of sea,
they dash off through the brine.

Round and round in circles
after mackerel they glide;
with the sun glinting on their shiny backs,
they take a sudden dive.

Then off they all fly, back out to sea,
leaving eye-straining tourists, breathless with glee.

Barbara Hepworth's garden is a truly amazing place to visit. Although we were in the middle of St Ives, I felt as though I had been transported to another place and another time.

The juxtaposition of sculpture and plants in the garden is magical, and each complements the other perfectly. It felt as if they understood each other thoroughly and had worked together to form the ideal landscape, which is why I called this poem 'A Conversation Between Sculpture and Leaf'.

A Conversation Between Sculpture and Leaf

Rising out of the shade
on a path to the ancient world
stained an industrial green,
erect figures tower,
proud and angular,
up through a verdant screen.

Smooth curves circle in harmony
to a mystical music of light,
the vibrant hum of the planets.
A copper coloured coolness
suffused in leafy shade,
perfection on a pedestal.

Chancing on a new civilisation,
bold amongst the ferns,
whispering to each other
through straight, clean lines,
a geometric extension
of the natural world.

St Ives by Night

A tale of two poems...One... Looking through my poems about St Ives, my dad asked if I would write one for him about St Ives by night. He loves St Ives in the evening when he likes to walk through the streets soaking up the atmosphere, and watch and listen to people in the restaurants, in the pubs and down at the harbour quay.

Early Morning in St Ives

A tale of two poems...Two...Having written a poem about St Ives by night, I started to think about St Ives in the early morning, when I like to wander through the town and along The Wharf, before the crowds appear. I love this time of day, when there are only a few people up and about – making deliveries, taking the dog for a walk, tidying up and making everything ready for when the tourists arrive.

The air and light have a special quality at this time in the morning, before the heat of the day descends on the town.

St Ives by Night

The scrape of contented
cutlery slips across
the empty plates;
and the crystal clinks
of wine glasses
toast a holiday success.

Harbour lights start to
gather, wobbling out
across the bay;
a cavalcade of
colour shimmers
out towards the sea.

Peering through a
window, from darkness
into light,
a flush of
smiling faces,
grinning over pints.

The plashing slap
of water against
the solid harbour wall;
a sudden shout,
an answering cry,
a throbbing motor dies.

The last train,
in the distance, clinging
gingerly to the cliff;
an arrow line
of scurrying lights
curving swiftly round the night.

A hush amongst
the secret streets,
the wind drops to a breath;
a drunken couple
reeling home,
as silence stirs the town.

Early Morning in St Ives

The newly drenched drip
of heavy hanging baskets.

The soft morning light
brushes shyly against
the harbour quay
as the town slips slowly
from shadow into sun.

The litter picker snaps
severely at cans and bottles.

Sights, sounds and smells
sharpen suddenly
into focus
fixed by the daze
of the warming sun.

The clear as crystal cries
of the early morning swimmers.

A cool, calm quiet,
a frisson in the air;
a piquant freshness
slowly smothered
by the rising heat.

The pasty vans cram
the soon to be bustling streets

One beautiful, warm September day Peter and I walked from our flat on the harbour front to Clodgy Point. The world seemed so alive - the sky a deep blue and the sea an almost tropical turquoise. There was, however, a slight hint in the air that autumn was starting to edge its way in.

We took it in turns to point out things that caught our eye as we walked along, and I noted these down and wrote the poem as soon as we got back. It is therefore a slightly disjointed image of St Ives based on our somewhat strange and side-ways view of looking at life. I hope you recognise your own picture of St Ives in it somewhere!

A September Day in St Ives

Crusted cream and Clodgy Point,
juvenile seagulls peep;
Idlehour on deckchair stripes,
slime-green trails of rope.

Red flags in the morning, bathers' warning.

Skeletal sea-thrift, purged of pink
edges over the cliff;
seed fluff, seed cups,
gorse-spike blackbirds' beaks.

Huge hydrangea heads like old ladies' swimming caps.

Ice green sea and dimpled sand,
fresh seabass and Parmesan mash;
holding hands across the sands,
berries brambling on the path.

Graves galore, sliding down towards the shore.

Waspish Sea King patrols the skies,
cat amongst the rocks;
sea-salt air on a tandoori breeze,
blank domino-eyed houses watch.

To the lighthouse!

The surfers never seem perturbed by the weather as
we saw one March afternoon at Porthmeor beach.

The sky was lead grey, the sea a forbidding mass of
cold, dark water. Coming round the Island we were
surprised by the sight of surfers in the distance,
crawling around like black beetles in the vast sea.

This poem was inspired by their persistence on a day
when we were wrapped up tightly, struggling against
the wind.

Surf's Up

Like sleek black seals
the surfers amass
under a threatening sky.

Stark silhouettes
they start to stir,
shifting with the swell.

Black dots bobbing
in a slate-grey sea,
awaiting the perfect wave.

Like an army of ants
the surfers swarm,
determined, towards the beach.

Perception is everything. When my husband read this poem he said, *'No, no, it wasn't like that at all!"* He remembered the evening perfectly well: the fishermen (and one lady) coming in from a day's fishing to unload their boats. He hadn't remembered, or rather hadn't noticed, however, all the cameras, the man excitedly filming, or me remarking that no one would want to come to my work and film me!

He remembered the fishermen themselves rather than the people on the periphery; the sudden flurry of activity, the surge of concentrated energy, the change from inaction to action, and hadn't even noticed the crowd milling round expectantly.

I hope, however, I have captured the scene as I saw it: the crowd jostling for position, wanting a better view; and the fishermen carrying on regardless, a measured and businesslike approach to their work.

At the End of the Day

The fishermen guide
their small boats in,
watched by an expectant crowd.
Cameras flashing
from side to side,
piercing through the dark.

A paparazzi of tourists
clicking furiously away,
filming the fishermen work.
Getting in the way,
milling in and out,
as the men unload their catch.

A flash of lurid light
on a well tanned face,
a shout to the next boat in.
The excitement rises
as crates are hauled up
and dumped on the harbour side.

I wonder if
they find it strange,
as they're hosing down their decks:
that buzz of delight,
the thrill of the crowd,
their momentary brush with fame.

Look out for the seal in the harbour – he (I think!) is usually there every day, especially when the fishing boats come in. I could watch him for hours, popping up and down. There is, however, something unsettling and slightly uncomfortable about watching him beg for fish from the fishermen.

In this poem I have tried to show that although the seal looks cute and sweet (which he does!) and may seem tame, he is still a wild and unpredictable creature at heart.

Harbour Seal

There is a certain appeal to the Grey Atlantic seal
as he begs for a mackerel fish.
With lugubrious eyes and mournful sighs
he haunts the boats returning

With excited zeal, a child chucks an eel;
the sand eel spirals downwards.
The seal dives below, direct as an arrow
but disdains so easy a free meal.

With a silvery flash, a mackerel makes a dash
into the oily waters.
With a curvaceous glide, under the water seal slides,
dark shadow under the surface sea-skin.

A periscope head rises up from the depths,
as he heaves himself up out the water.
Puffing and blowing like an old man toiling,
snorting through his twitching whiskers.

With a jerk of the head, a vicious twist of the neck,
he throws himself hard at the water.
A telltale sign, of the wild creature inside
behind the black mooning soul-eyes.

There is a seat at Porthgwidden beach that Peter and I sit on each evening as the stars begin to come out. The lapping of the waves on the shore and the stillness of the night air makes it the perfect romantic spot, and a place to sit and let the atmosphere wash over you.

This poem was inspired by the full moon that dominated the night sky as we sat there one evening in September.

Moon Over Porthgwidden

A furrow of shivering moonlight
slicks across the oil black sea
and over the silvered satin sand.

Mooning circle coins the dark night sky,
single satellite star in tow,
brushing the furry cloud surround.

Follow the silver brick road of light,
parting of the seas
opens up the depths of night.

Having visited St Ives on several occasions now, at different times of the year and at different times of day and night, I have seen and felt the sea in many of its different moods and this poem tries to capture some of these.

Sea Moods

A tiny light, pinprick bright,
steadfast in the pitch-black sea.
A line of lights, holds back the night
in silent single file.

Azure blue day, reflects the bay,
glittering sparkles of light;
bobbing about, a bumbling crowd:
a splash of red and white.

Foaming flecks, sun bleached decks,
weaving in and out;
dashing boldly along, a speeding throng,
clipping on the racing breeze.

Dark slate grey, the waves obey
the grim grey skies above;
tossed high and low, against the flow,
a cold, hard wall of water.

Newly laundered blue
a pale, soft hue
a seagull cries
airlifts high
calm all around
gravelly sound
soft push and pull
against the hull
gentle lap
sail-beat flap
sky meets sea
blurs reality
rise
fall
ebb
flow
single grain of sand
dissolved land.

We actually saw the mermaid of Zennor. We took the bus to Zennor one morning and started to walk back along the coast to St Ives. Just over half way, and while I was in the middle of a moan about how long it was taking, we saw her in the water, quite near to the cliffs, bathing in a cove. She must have seen us as well because she was off, swimming close to the coast, and soon disappeared out of sight.

This poem is her story.

The Mermaid of Zennor

Hugging the coast tightly,
her shiny body
undulates with the water,
revelling in
the joy of swimming:
curving and gliding,
flexing and winding
in amongst the waves.

Picking up speed,
she slips through
the sea-stream,
an envious eye
always on the coastline;
swirling and curling,
surging and merging
in amongst the waves.

Is she lonely,
I wonder,
the last one left,
alone for the past hundred years?
When the last of her kin
was enmeshed in a net,
caught threshing
in airtight agony.

Does she mind,
I wonder,
as she flashes by
in a glint of blinding sunlight,
having only the sea
to hear her thoughts,
to share her
innermost secrets?

Spawned in sea
in a flurry of froth,
deep in the
heart of the ocean,
she remains forever prey
to the ever-shifting moods
of an ever-restless,
ever-changing sea.

Gravelly voice soothing,
boiling frenzy seething,
soft crooning,
cruel raging,
splash and plash,
roar and crash:
she is cruelly dashed against the rocks,
then gently rocked to sleep.

Hugging the coast tightly,
her shiny body
undulates with the water;
an envious eye
always on the coastline,
a fearful eye always on the sea;
but luxuriating in
the joy of swimming,
she accepts the price of
her watery thraldom
and banishes all thought
of ever being free.